1. How many lakes are in Alaska?

A. 3 million
B. 516
C. 200
D. 1 million

2. How many countries are part of Great Britain?

A. 3
B. 4
C. 5
D. 2

3. What was branch of science was Ernest Rutherford famous for?

A. botany
B. meteorology
C. paleontology
D. radioactivity

4. What country was formerly called Siam?

A. Laos
B. Indonesia
C. Iran
D. Thailand

5. Where is the Sea of Tranquility located?

   A. Mars
   B. Earth
   C. Jupiter
   D. The moon

6. Who painted the Mona Lisa?

   A. Michelangelo
   B. Leonardo da Vinci
   C. Edgar Degas
   D. Raphael

7. What bird can remember bad memories for up to 5 years?

   A. Kiwis
   B. Parrots
   C. Crows
   D. Sparrows

8. What did Alexander Fleming famously discover?

   A. DNA
   B. gravity
   C. penicillin
   D. vaccinations

9. In Roman Myth Mars is the god of what?

A. Games
B. love
C. war
D. law

10. What was Hugh Hefner's jet plane named?

A. Bad Bunny
B. Pretty Bunny
C. Big Bunny
D. Sweet Bunny

11. What's the most populous city in the United States?

A. New York City
B. Los Angeles
C. Chicago
D. Houston

12. What year was the Seneca Falls Convention?

A. 1845
B. 1830
C. 1848
D. 138

13. What is the official and current name of Big Ben?

A. Clock Tower
B. Bell Tower
C. Elizabeth Tower
D. Victoria Tower

14. Which country has the longest coastline?

A. Canada
B. Kuwait
C. Guam
D. India

15. Where would you find the smallest bones in the human body?

A. ear
B. finger
C. spine
D. toe

16. The penny-farthing was a popular type of what?

A. Hula-hoop
B. Flute
C. Bicycle
D. Dance

17. What was the first source of Roman Law?

A. 12 tables
B. 13 tables
C. Pax Romana
D. mos maiorum

18. Who had the nickname Scarface?

A. Truman Capote
B. Elliot Ness
C. Al Capone
D. Bugsy Siegel

19. Which was the largest tank battle in history?

A. Somme
B. Britain
C. Kursk
D. Stalingrad

20. What is the capital of Indonesia?

A. Medan
B. Makassar
C. Jakarta
D. Yogyakarta

21. The Inca Trail is found in which country?

A. Estonia
B. Somalia
C. Peru
D. Cuba

22. What is the longest river in Australia?

A. The Murray River
B. The Darling River
C. Lachlan River
D. Cooper Creek

23. What was discovered in the Yukon in 1896?

A. Dinosaur fossils
B. gold
C. oil
D. ancient tribe

24. What is the name for the monetary unit used in Thailand?

A. Dollar
B. Dinar
C. Bhat
D. Real

25. Carrots are a good source of which vitamin?

A. Vitamin C
B. Vitamin B
C. Vitamin E
D. Vitamin A

26. Which city lies on two continents?

A. Istanbul
B. Baghdad
C. Bursa
D. Adana

27. Which planet has the strongest gravitational force?

A. Earth
B. Jupiter
C. Mercury
D. Uranus

28. How many hearts does a worm have?

A. 1
B. 2
C. 3
D. 5

29. According to Greek myth who had snakes for hair?

A. Medusa
B. Venus
C. Artemia
D. Aphrodite

30. What was the Louvre in Paris before it became a Museum?

A. Government Building
B. Courthouse
C. Palace
D. University

31. Mesopotamia is now called as?

A. Iraq
B. Saudi Arabia
C. Turkey
D. Tanzania

32. The kiwi is native to which country?

A. Australia
B. Solomon Islands
C. New Zealand
D. Fiji

33. Which among these countries is still led by a monarch?

A. Saudi Arabia
B. Egypt
C. Portugal
D. France

34. Where would you find the Yangtze River?

A. India
B. China
C. Indonesia
D. Papua New Guinea

35. Who discovered King Tut's tomb?

A. Henry Wilson
B. Howard Carter
C. Charles Smith
D. Edward Peters

36. How many games did Ken Griffey Jr. and his father play together?

A. 51
B. 12
C. 2
D. 7

37. What is the currency of Japan?

A. yen
B. won
C. dollar
D. krone

38. Where was the U.S. largest surrender in battle?

A. Bataan
B. Berlin
C. Paris
D. Tokyo

39. Which of these animals lays eggs?

A. bat
B. echidna
C. hedgehog
D. pangolin

40. What was France originally called?

A. Gaul
B. Lutetia
C. Lyon
D. Merea

41. Which country has cross country skiing as its national sport?

A. Japan
B. USA
C. Norway
D. Switzerland

42. How many countries have names that end in -stan?

A. 10
B. 5
C. 8
D. 7

43. Which of these substances is acidic?

A. ammonia
B. limewater
C. soap
D. vinegar

44. In which city does the queen live?

A. London
B. Edinburgh
C. Manchester
D. Bristol

45. How many Theses did Martine Luther write?

A. 99
B. 100
C. 90
D. 95

46. Which are the safest countries for travellers?

A. Iceland
B. Australia
C. India
D. South Korea

47. How many republics were part of the Soviet Union?

A. 12
B. 20
C. 15
D. 10

48. The longest rail in the world starts in which city?

A. Moscow
B. Beijing
C. Mumbai
D. Surat

49. The Eiffel Tower was originally intended for what city?

A. Madrid
B. Marseille
C. Milan
D. Barcelona

50. Parmesan cheese originated from which country?

A. France
B. USA
C. Belgium
D. Italy

51. The term malar refers to what part of the human body?

A. cheek
B. feet
C. lung
D. toes

52. Which gas is makes up around 78% of the air we breathe?

A. carbon dioxide
B. hydrogen
C. oxygen
D. nitrogen

53. Cirque du Soleil started in what country?

A. Canada
B. France
C. Italy
D. Mexico

54. What US state shares a border with Canada?

A. North Dakota
B. Texas
C. North Carolina
D. Nevada

55. How long is a jiffy?

A. 22 minutes
B. One trillionth of a second
C. A quarter of a second
D. 772.4 mph

56. Which bird has the largest wingspan of any living bird?

A. The Great Red Hawk
B. Blakiston's Fish Owl
C. The wandering albatross
D. Andean Condor

57. Which planet is the hottest in the solar system?

A. Venus
B. Mercury
C. Jupiter
D. Mars

58. Which president is responsible for the forward pass?

A. William Howard Taft
B. William McKinley
C. Teddy Roosevelt
D. Franklin D. Roosevelt

59. The Paris Peace Accords ended which conflict?

A. WWI
B. WWII
C. Vietnam War
D. Korean War

60. Which country invented paper?

A. China
B. Japan
C. USA
D. Spain

61. What color is a polar bear's skin?

A. Black
B. Brown
C. White
D. Spotted

62. In which U.S. state was the atomic bomb tested in?

A. New York
B. New Mexico
C. Nevada
D. Texas

63. An ohm is a measure of what?

A. current
B. power
C. resistance
D. voltage

64. Amino acids are the building blocks of which molecules?

A. carbohydrates
B. lipids
C. proteins
D. sugars

65. Which U.S. President had a pet parrot?

A. Jackson
B. Wilson
C. Adams
D. Lincoln

66. Which nuts are used to make marzipan?

A. Almonds
B. Walnuts
C. Pine nuts
D. Cashews

67. In electricity - what does the abbreviation AC stand for?

A. alternating circuit
B. alternating charge
C. alternating current
D. alternative current

68. How many ribs are in a human body?

A. 16
B. 28
C. 22
D. Twenty-four

69. How many noses does a slug have?

A. Two
B. Three
C. None
D. Four

70. The Petronas Towers is located in what country?

A. Singapore
B. Indonesia
C. Thailand
D. Malaysia

71. Where in your body is your axilla?

A. ankle
B. armpit
C. ear
D. knee

72. Florence Nightingale was a nurse in which war?

A. Crimean War
B. WWI
C. WWII
D. Klang War

73. Who invented the cotton gin?

A. Eli Whitney
B. Thomas Edison
C. Henry Ford
D. Thomas Jefferson

74. Who was the mother of Queen Elizabeth I?

A. Anne Boleyn
B. Elizabeth Blount
C. Catherine Parr
D. Jane Grey

75. What is the function of a xylem in a plant?

A. nutrient storage
B. reproduction
C. photosynthesis
D. transport of water

76. In which of Britney's video does she appear as a stewardess?

A. ... Baby One More Time
B. Womanizer
C. Toxic
D. Pretty Girls

77. What did J. Edgar Hoover not want people walking on?

A. His legacy
B. His dropped cigarette butts
C. His words
D. His shadow

78. Which country did Winston Churchill lead during WWII?

A. U.K
B. Canada
C. Spain
D. France

79. Where is the Stone Henge located?

A. England
B. Netherlands
C. Pakistan
D. Brazil

80. Who is the youngest player ever to hit 500 home runs?

A. Gary Sheffield
B. Alex Rodriguez
C. Jimmie Foxx
D. David Ortiz

81. What is the first element on the Periodic Table?

A. Oxygen
B. Calcium
C. Iron
D. Hydrogen

82. Which country has the most number of islands?

A. Philippines
B. Sweden
C. Japan
D. Indonesia

83. Port-au-Prince is the capital of which country?

A. Dominican Republic
B. Haiti
C. Suriname
D. Grenada

84. Where do natural pearls comes from?

A. ice
B. rock ore
C. oysters
D. whales

85. Which country has the highest number of tourists yearly?

A. Japan
B. France
C. Thailand
D. Greece

86. What is the name of the Earth's largest ocean?

A. Pacific Ocean
B. Atlantic Ocean
C. Artic Ocean
D. Indian Ocean

87. What is the common name for dried plums?

A. Raisans
B. Prunes
C. Kumquats
D. Kiwi

88. Who was the first performer at the Woodstock festival in 1969?

A. Joan Baez
B. Richie Havens
C. Joe Cocker
D. Santana

89. Who established the 365-day calendar?

A. Augustus
B. Julius Caesar
C. Trajan
D. Henry VI

90. Hepatitis is inflammation of which organ?

A. brain
B. kidney
C. liver
D. lung

91. Which country has never lost a war?

A. Pakistan
B. North Korea
C. Israel
D. USA

92. What is the capital of Romania?

A. Asuncion
B. Belfast
C. Rabat
D. Bucharest

93. Where in your body might you find alveoli?

A. colon
B. heart
C. lungs
D. stomach

94. Where do the Grimm's fairy tales originate from?

A. Germany
B. France
C. Russia
D. Netherlands

95. Why are hockey pucks frozen before a game?

A. To prevent their breaking up
B. To prevent them from bouncing
C. To add strength
D. To prevent injuries to players

96. What is the most abundant metal in the Earth's crust?

A. Iron
B. Lead
C. Aluminium
D. Sodium

97. What is the largest planet in our solar system?

A. Saturn
B. Jupiter
C. Venus
D. Neptune

98. Which country has the lowest crime rate?

A. Canada
B. Iceland
C. USA
D. Bolivia

99. In Texas it's illegal to swear in front of what?

A. A child
B. A horse
C. A sheriff
D. A corpse

100. What is allspice alternatively known as?

A. Garlic
B. Pimento
C. Saffron
D. Thyme

101. In what year was the first iPhone released?

A. 2005
B. 2007
C. 2009
D. 2010

102. Name the only New York Yankee to hit four home runs in one game?

A. Ty Cobb
B. Joe DiMaggio
C. Micky Mantle
D. Lou Gehrig

103. In what country would one compete in a wife carry race?

A. Sweden
B. Denmark
C. Finland
D. Norway

104. What is the capital city of Canada's Yukon territory?

A. Edmonton
B. Whitehorse
C. Banff
D. Moose Jaw

105. How many people have walked on the moon?

A. 2
B. 8
C. 12
D. 21

106. What is the deepest lake in the world?

A. Lake Michigan
B. Lake Victoria
C. Lake Vostok
D. Lake Baikal

107. Which type of fruit juice did Dole sell first?

A. Cranberry
B. Pineapple
C. Grape
D. Tomato

108. What is the unit of electrical current?

A. amp
B. ohm
C. volt
D. watt

109. A riel is the currency of which country?

A. Kyrgyzstan
B. Mongolia
C. Cambodia
D. Myanmar

110. Which Theatre did Shakespeare create?

A. London Theatre
B. Global Theatre
C. Globe Theatre
D. Essex Theatre

111. Louis Pasteur is credited with the discovery of what?

A. DNA
B. pasteurization
C. penicillin
D. x-rays

112. Who discovered the Rosetta Stone?

A. Napoleon
B. French Solider
C. Thomas Young
D. Doug Fields

113. Where did Barack Obama teach constitutional law?

A. University of Chicago
B. University of Illinois
C. Northwestern University
D. Loyola University

114. Complete the title of a 1979 number one by Blondie Heart of...

A. Glass
B. Gold
C. Platinum
D. Steel

115. What was Cleopatra's nationality?

A. Mesopotamian
B. Greek. Egyptian
C. Macedonian
D. Macedonian

116. What was the first state?

A. Delaware
B. New Jersey
C. Vermont
D. Virginia

117. Which city was the U.S. capital from 1785-1790?

A. Boston
B. New York
C. Chicago
D. Denver

118. Who was the first U.S Secretary of Treasury?

A. Alexander Hamilton
B. John Adams
C. Aaron Burr
D. Thomas Edison

119. The Warren Spahn Award is given to:

A. Best left-handed pitcher
B. Most outstanding designated hitter
C. Best pitcher of the season
D. Top hitter in each league

120. Who signed the Magna Carta?

A. King George
B. King William
C. King John
D. Queen Victoria

121. Who invented the radio?

A. Alexander Graham Bell
B. Thomas Edison
C. Philo Taylor Farnsworth
D. Guglielmo Marconi

122. Which is the world's highest waterfall?

A. Kunchikal Falls
B. Ribbon Fall
C. Angel Falls
D. Yosemite Falls

123. Which country was Joan of Arc from?

A. Russia
B. Italy
C. England
D. France

124. Juba is the capital of which country?

A. Vietnam
B. Yemen
C. South Sudan
D. Sierra Leone

125. Which river flows through the Grand Canyon?

A. Colorado River
B. Missouri River
C. Yukon River
D. Rio Grande

126. Which among these countries do NOT border Italy?

A. France
B. Vatican City
C. San Marino
D. Belgium

127. Which ocean is the Bermuda Triangle located?

A. North Atlantic
B. Pacific
C. Indian
D. Arctic

128. Around how many countries have a royal family?

A. 12
B. 25
C. 43
D. 5

129. Which sea is located in Israel and Jordan?

A. Dead Sea
B. Red Sea
C. Arabian Sea
D. Sea of Sand

130. Which country offered Albert Einstein presidency?

A. Germany
B. Austria
C. Israel
D. Poland

131. Roger Federer holds the citizenship of which two nations?

A. Switzerland and South Africa
B. Switzerland and Portugal
C. Switzerland and Austria
D. Switzerland and Norway

132. In Alaska it's legal to shoot bears but illegal to do what?

A. Scare one
B. Chase one
C. Yell at one
D. Wake one up

133. Who designed the current U.S flag?

A. Robert Borden
B. Robert Heft
C. Daniel Peterson
D. Bill Young

134. In which branch of the arts is Katherine Dunham famous?

A. Interpretive Dance
B. Tap dancing
C. Performance Arts
D. Ballet

135. What number did Derek Jeter wear on his New York Yankees jersey?

A. 4
B. 11
C. 2
D. 7

136. An Apgar score is given to what?

A. Graduate students
B. Health of newborns
C. Velocity of an object in a vacuum
D. Acidity in drinks

137. What is the most abundant element in the universe?

A. Hydrogen
B. Oxygen
C. Carbon
D. Neon

138. What was Harry Houdini's real name?

A. Erik Weisz
B. Aaron Wein
C. Harry Weisz
D. Harry Truman

139. King Henry VI of England was also the king of which country?

A. Spain
B. Italy
C. France
D. Russia

140. What unit of measurement is equal to 4047 square meters?

A. acre
B. hectare
C. square kilometer
D. square mile

141. Name the team with the most Super Bowl appearances?

A. Buffalo Bills
B. New England Patriots
C. Dallas Cowboys
D. Pittsburgh Steelers

142. Which dinosaur had 15 horns?

A. Koreaceratops
B. Kosmoceratops
C. Pachyrhinosaurus
D. Protoceratops

143. What is the most abundant element in the known universe?

A. carbon
B. hydrogen
C. iron
D. nitrogen

144. Which New York Yankee player was nicknamed the "Yankee Clipper"?

A. Joe DiMaggio
B. Mickey Mantle
C. Whitey Ford
D. Roger Maris

145. What did the Olympics used to award medals for?

A. Art
B. Singing
C. Writing
D. Speaking

146. Which King of England broke apart from the Catholic Church?

A. John
B. Henry VIII
C. Charles II
D. George

147. Why did Rosa Parks get arrested?

A. Refusal to give her seat
B. protesting
C. attending a Sit-in
D. stealing

148. Dutch people live in which country?

A. Georgia
B. Netherlands
C. Belgium
D. Denmark

149. Which disease did the Spanish bring to the Aztec empire?

A. Black Death
B. smallpox
C. influenza
D. malaria

150. What does the word Matrix mean in the Bible?

A. Womb
B. Burial place
C. Heaven
D. Prophet

151. Which country has the most mountains?

A. India
B. USA
C. China
D. Russia

152. Who wrote songs for The Lion King?

A. Elton John
B. Billy Joel
C. Paul McCartney
D. Stevie Wonder

153. Who was the first mascot of the Cincinnati Reds baseball team?

A. Mr. Redlegs
B. Mr. Red
C. Gapper
D. Paws

154. Napoleon suffered defeat at Waterloo in what year?

A. 1812
B. 1833
C. 1815
D. 1801

155. In Denmark what is a Svangerskabsforebyggendemiddel?

A. A type of fermented fish
B. A sock made from alpaca fur
C. A condom
D. A milky drink

156. What is the largest type of deer?

A. Bull
B. Moose
C. Stag
D. Big Antler

157. What was the first name of the first American born saint?

A. Anne
B. Martha
C. Elizabeth
D. Paul

158. What big event happened in London in 1666?

A. Wedding
B. fire
C. battle
D. natural disaster

159. What is the tiny piece at the end of a shoelace called?

A. Aglet
B. Edge
C. Clasp
D. Catch

160. Canberra is the capital city of which country?

A. New Zealand
B. Australia
C. Papau New Guinea
D. Fiji

161. Other than a General what was Stonewall Jackson other career?

A. Carpentry
B. lawyer
C. teacher
D. merchant

162. Which city is shared by two countries?

A. Luxembourg
B. Seville
C. Granada
D. Marseille

163. Marilyn Monroe was married to which famous sportsman?

A. Yogi Berra
B. Justin Verlander
C. Ralph Kiner
D. Joe DiMaggio

164. What is the softest mineral in the world?

A. Diamond
B. Calcite
C. Talc
D. Apatite

165. The Cold War was between the U.S. and which country?

A. Italy
B. England
C. Germany
D. Russia

166. What is the most populous city in Canada?

A. Vancouver
B. Toronto
C. Montreal
D. Quebec City

167. What language has the most words?

A. French
B. English
C. Chinese
D. Hindi

168. The Claret Jug is presented to the winner of which tournament?

A. Masters Tournament
B. The Open Championship
C. PGA Championship
D. U.S. Open

169. In Georgia, it's illegal to eat what with a fork?

A. Macaroni
B. Potato salad
C. Fried chicken
D. Okra

170. The coldest place on Earth is located in which continent?

A. Antarctica
B. North America
C. Asia
D. South America

171. Who developed the theory of relativity?

A. Marie Curie
B. Albert Einstein
C. Stephen Hawking
D. Isaac Newton

172. Which is the northernmost country?

A. Greenland
B. Mongolia
C. Iceland
D. U.K.

173. The lack of which vitamin can result in scurvy?

A. Vitamin A
B. Vitamin C
C. Vitamin D
D. Vitamin K

174. Who was the Iron Lady?

A. Theresa May
B. Meryl Streep
C. Margaret Thatcher
D. Carol Thatcher

175. Who was the first person to suggest Daylight Savings Times?

A. Benjamin Franklin
B. Adam Smith
C. George Washington
D. Thomas Jefferson

176. How many states are there in the USA?

A. 60
B. 50
C. 32
D. 49

177. Which country uses the most renewable energy?

A. Iceland
B. Spain
C. Ireland
D. Finland

178. Which gas makes the bubbles in a soda drink?

A. argon
B. carbon dioxide
C. nitrogen
D. oxygen

179. What was the first mammal to be sent into space?

A. dog
B. guinea pig
C. monkey
D. mouse

180. Where were the fortune cookies invented?

A. San Francisco
B. Shanghai
C. Tokyo
D. Busan

181. Which colour has the highest frequency in the visible spectrum?

A. blue
B. indigo
C. red
D. violet

182. Which country has the highest agricultural production?

A. China
B. Brazil
C. Australia
D. Russia

183. What is dendrochronology?

A. climate science
B. study of skin
C. study of teeth
D. tree-ring dating

184. Which country is the biggest?

A. India
B. Japan
C. Thailand
D. Singapore

185. Who did Aaron Burr kill?

A. Abraham Lincoln
B. Alexander Hamilton
C. George Washington
D. Thomas Jefferson

186. How did Fredrick Douglass escape slavery?

A. Ran away
B. underground railroad
C. disguised as a sailor
D. murder

187. How many time zones does Russia span?

A. 6
B. 7
C. 11
D. 15

188. How many karats is pure gold?

A. 10
B. 14
C. 24
D. 30

189. Which franchise has won the most championships in the NBA?

A. Minneapolis Lakers
B. Los Angeles Lakers
C. Boston Celtics
D. San Antonio Spurs

190. Which civilization invented the wheel?

A. Egypt
B. China
C. Rome
D. Mesopotamia

191. Danish people live in which country?

A. Denmark
B. Slovenia
C. Dominican Republic
D. Hungary

192. How many signs are there in the Zodiac?

A. 10
B. 12
C. 8
D. 14

193. Who wrote Frankenstein?

A. Mary Shelley
B. Percy Shelley
C. Franklin Stein
D. Howard Young

194. Abbey Road is located in which city?

A. Leeds
B. Nottingham
C. London
D. Bristol

195. Which bone are babies born without?

A. A Rib
B. Elbow
C. Thigh Bone
D. Knee cap

196. What is someone who shoes horses?

A. A ferrier
B. A farrier
C. A farber
D. A harrier

197. What country was formerly called Ceylon?

A. Tanzania
B. Sri Lanka
C. Haiti
D. Canada

198. How long is New Zealand's Ninety Mile Beach?

A. 91 miles
B. 64 miles
C. 45 miles
D. 55 miles

199. What is the name for the group of men who elect a Pope?

A. College of Bishops
B. Meeting of Cardinals
C. Meeting of Ministers
D. College of Cardinals

200. What are the two fruit juices in a cosmopolitan?

A. Cranberry and lemon
B. Orange and cranberry
C. Cranberry and lime
D. Pineapple and coconut

1. How many lakes are in Alaska?

3 million

2. How many countries are part of Great Britain?

3

3. What was branch of science was Ernest Rutherford famous for?

Radioactivity

4. What country was formerly called Siam?

Thailand

5. Where is the Sea of Tranquility located?

The moon

6. Who painted the Mona Lisa?

Leonardo da Vinci

7. What bird can remember bad memories for up to 5 years?

Kiwis

8. What did Alexander Fleming famously discover?

Penicillin

9. In Roman Myth Mars is the god of what?

war

10. What was Hugh Hefner's jet plane named?

Big Bunny

11. What's the most populous city in the United States?

New York City

12. What year was the Seneca Falls Convention?

1848

13. What is the official and current name of Big Ben?

Elizabeth Tower

14. Which country has the longest coastline?

Canada

15. Where would you find the smallest bones in the human body?

Ear

16. The penny-farthing was a popular type of what?

Bicycle

17. What was the first source of Roman Law?

12 tables

18. Who had the nickname Scarface?

Al Capone

19. Which was the largest tank battle in history?

Kursk

20. What is the capital of Indonesia?

Jakarta

21. The Inca Trail is found in which country?

Peru

22. What is the longest river in Australia?

The Murray River

23. What was discovered in the Yukon in 1896?

gold

24. What is the name for the monetary unit used in Thailand?

Thai Bhat

25. Carrots are a good source of which vitamin?

Vitamin A

26. Which city lies on two continents?

Istanbul

27. Which planet has the strongest gravitational force?

Jupiter

28. How many hearts does a worm have?

5

29. According to Greek myth who had snakes for hair?

Medusa

30. What was the Louvre in Paris before it became a Museum?

Palace

31. Mesopotamia is now called as?

Iraq

32. The kiwi is native to which country?

New Zealand

33. Which among these countries is still led by a monarch?

Saudi Arabia

34. Where would you find the Yangtze River?

China

35. Who discovered King Tut's tomb?

Howard Carter

36. How many games did Ken Griffey Jr. and his father play together?

51

37. What is the currency of Japan?

yen

38. Where was the U.S. largest surrender in battle?

Bataan

39. Which of these animals lays eggs?

Echidna

40. What was France originally called?

Gaul

41. Which country has cross country skiing as its national sport?

Norway

42. How many countries have names that end in -stan?

7

43. Which of these substances is acidic?

Vinegar

44. In which city does the queen live?

London

45. How many Theses did Martine Luther write?

95

46. Which are the safest countries for travellers?

Iceland

47. How many republics were part of the Soviet Union?

15

48. The longest rail in the world starts in which city?

Moscow

49. The Eiffel Tower was originally intended for what city?

Barcelona

50. Parmesan cheese originated from which country?

Italy

51. The term malar refers to what part of the human body?

Cheek

52. Which gas is makes up around 78% of the air we breathe?

Nitrogen

53. Cirque du Soleil started in what country?

Canada

54. What US state shares a border with Canada?

North Dakota

55. How long is a jiffy?

One trillionth of a second

56. Which bird has the largest wingspan of any living bird?

The wandering albatross

57. Which planet is the hottest in the solar system?

Venus

58. Which president is responsible for the forward pass?

Teddy Roosevelt

59. The Paris Peace Accords ended which conflict?

Vietnam War

60. Which country invented paper?

China

61. What color is a polar bear's skin?

Black

62. In which U.S. state was the atomic bomb tested in?

New Mexico

63. An ohm is a measure of what?

Resistance

64. Amino acids are the building blocks of which molecules?

Proteins

65. Which U.S. President had a pet parrot?

Jackson

66. Which nuts are used to make marzipan?

Almonds

67. In electricity - what does the abbreviation AC stand for?

Alternating current

68. How many ribs are in a human body?

Twenty-four

69. How many noses does a slug have?

Four

70. The Petronas Towers is located in what country?

Malaysia

71. Where in your body is your axilla?

Armpit

72. Florence Nightingale was a nurse in which war?

Crimean War

73. Who invented the cotton gin?

Eli Whitney

74. Who was the mother of Queen Elizabeth I?

Anne Boleyn

75. What is the function of a xylem in a plant?

Transport of water

76. In which of Britney's video does she appear as a stewardess?

Toxic

77. What did J. Edgar Hoover not want people walking on?

His shadow

78. Which country did Winston Churchill lead during WWII?

U.K.

79. Where is the Stone Henge located?

England

80. Who is the youngest player ever to hit 500 home runs?

Alex Rodriguez

81. What is the first element on the Periodic Table?

Hydrogen

82. Which country has the most number of islands?

Sweden

83. Port-au-Prince is the capital of which country?

Haiti

84. Where do natural pearls comes from?

Oysters

85. Which country has the highest number of tourists yearly?

France

86. What is the name of the Earth's largest ocean?

The Pacific Ocean

87. What is the common name for dried plums?

Prunes

88. Who was the first performer at the Woodstock festival in 1969?

Richie Havens

89. Who established the 365-day calendar?

Julius Caesar

90. Hepatitis is inflammation of which organ?

Liver

91. Which country has never lost a war?

Pakistan

92. What is the capital of Romania?

Bucharest

93. Where in your body might you find alveoli?

Lungs

94. Where do the Grimm's fairy tales originate from?

Germany

95. Why are hockey pucks frozen before a game?

To prevent them from bouncing

96. What is the most abundant metal in the Earth's crust?

Aluminium

97. What is the largest planet in our solar system?

Jupiter

98. Which country has the lowest crime rate?

Iceland

99. In Texas it's illegal to swear in front of what?

A corpse

100. What is allspice alternatively known as?

Pimento

101. In what year was the first iPhone released?

2007

102. Name the only New York Yankee to hit four home runs in one game?

Lou Gehrig

103. In what country would one compete in a wife carry race?

Finland

104. What is the capital city of Canada's Yukon territory?

Whitehorse

105. How many people have walked on the moon?

12

106. What is the deepest lake in the world?

Lake Baikal

107. Which type of fruit juice did Dole sell first?

Pineapple

108. What is the unit of electrical current?

Amp

109. A riel is the currency of which country?

Cambodia

110. Which Theatre did Shakespeare create?

Globe Theatre

111. Louis Pasteur is credited with the discovery of what?

Pasteurization

112. Who discovered the Rosetta Stone?

French Soldier

113. Where did Barack Obama teach constitutional law?

University of Chicago

114. Complete the title of a 1979 number one by Blondie Heart of...

Glass

115. What was Cleopatra's nationality?

116. What was the first state?

Delaware

117. Which city was the U.S. capital from 1785-1790?

New York

118. Who was the first U.S Secretary of Treasury?

Alexander Hamilton

119. The Warren Spahn Award is given to:

Best left-handed pitcher

120. Who signed the Magna Carta?

King John

121. Who invented the radio?

Guglielmo Marconi

122. Which is the world's highest waterfall?

Angel Falls

123. Which country was Joan of Arc from?

France

124. Juba is the capital of which country?

South Sudan

125. Which river flows through the Grand Canyon?

Colorado River

126. Which among these countries do NOT border Italy?

Belgium

127. Which ocean is the Bermuda Triangle located?

North Atlantic

128. Around how many countries have a royal family?

43

129. Which sea is located in Israel and Jordan?

Dead Sea

130. Which country offered Albert Einstein presidency?

Israel

131. Roger Federer holds the citizenship of which two nations?

Switzerland and South Africa

132. In Alaska it's legal to shoot bears but illegal to do what?

Wake one up

133. Who designed the current U.S flag?

Robert Heft

134. In which branch of the arts is Katherine Dunham famous?

Ballet

135. What number did Derek Jeter wear on his New York Yankees jersey?

2

136. An Apgar score is given to what?

Health of newborns

137. What is the most abundant element in the universe?

Hydrogen

138. What was Harry Houdini's real name?

Erik Weisz

139. King Henry VI of England was also the king of which country?

France

140. What unit of measurement is equal to 4047 square meters?

Acre

141. Name the team with the most Super Bowl appearances?

New England Patriots

142. Which dinosaur had 15 horns?

Kosmoceratops

143. What is the most abundant element in the known universe?

Hydrogen

144. Which New York Yankee player was nicknamed the "Yankee Clipper"?

Joe DiMaggio

145. What did the Olympics used to award medals for?

Art

146. Which King of England broke apart from the Catholic Church?

Henry VIII

147. Why did Rosa Parks get arrested?

Refusal to give her seat

148. Dutch people live in which country?

Netherlands

149. Which disease did the Spanish bring to the Aztec empire?

smallpox

150. What does the word Matrix mean in the Bible?

Womb

151. Which country has the most mountains?

USA

152. Who wrote songs for The Lion King?

Elton John

153. Who was the first mascot of the Cincinnati Reds baseball team?

Mr. Red

154. Napoleon suffered defeat at Waterloo in what year?

1815

155. In Denmark what is a Svangerskabsforebyggendemiddel?

A condom

156. What is the largest type of deer?

Moose

157. What was the first name of the first American born saint?

Elizabeth

158. What big event happened in London in 1666?

fire

159. What is the tiny piece at the end of a shoelace called?

Aglet

160. Canberra is the capital city of which country?

Australia

161. Other than a General what was Stonewall Jackson other career?

teacher

162. Which city is shared by two countries?

Luxembourg

163. Marilyn Monroe was married to which famous sportsman?

Joe DiMaggio

164. What is the softest mineral in the world?

Talc

165. The Cold War was between the U.S. and which country?

Russia

166. What is the most populous city in Canada?

Toronto

167. What language has the most words?

English

168. The Claret Jug is presented to the winner of which tournament?

The Open Championship

169. In Georgia, it's illegal to eat what with a fork?

Fried chicken

170. The coldest place on Earth is located in which continent?

Antarctica

171. Who developed the theory of relativity?

Albert Einstein

172. Which is the northernmost country?

Greenland

173. The lack of which vitamin can result in scurvy?

Vitamin C

174. Who was the Iron Lady?

Margaret Thatcher

175. Who was the first person to suggest Daylight Savings Times?

Benjamin Franklin

176. How many states are there in the USA?

50

177. Which country uses the most renewable energy?

Iceland

178. Which gas makes the bubbles in a soda drink?

Carbon dioxide

179. What was the first mammal to be sent into space?

Monkey

180. Where were the fortune cookies invented?

San Francisco

181. Which colour has the highest frequency in the visible spectrum?

Violet

182. Which country has the highest agricultural production?

China

183. What is dendrochronology?

Tree-ring dating

184. Which country is the biggest?

India

185. Who did Aaron Burr kill?

Alexander Hamilton

186. How did Fredrick Douglass escape slavery?

disguised as a sailor

187. How many time zones does Russia span?

11

188. How many karats is pure gold?

24

189. Which franchise has won the most championships in the NBA?

Boston Celtics

190. Which civilization invented the wheel?

Mesopotamia

191. Danish people live in which country?

Denmark

192. How many signs are there in the Zodiac?

12

193. Who wrote Frankenstein?

Mary Shelley

194. Abbey Road is located in which city?

London

195. Which bone are babies born without?

Knee cap

196. What is someone who shoes horses?

A farrier

197. What country was formerly called Ceylon?

Sri Lanka

198. How long is New Zealand's Ninety Mile Beach?

55 miles

199. What is the name for the group of men who elect a Pope?

College of Cardinals

200. What are the two fruit juices in a cosmopolitan?

Cranberry and lime

www.ingramcontent.com/pod-product-compliance
Ingram Content Group UK Ltd.
Pitfield, Milton Keynes, MK11 3LW, UK
UKHW061828190726
13853UKWH00009B/2506

9 798707 247866